The V

by David McCullough

: THIS IS A QUICK READ SUMMARY BASED ON THE BOOK "THE WRIGHT BROTHERS" BY DAVID MCCULLOUGH

NOTE TO READERS:

This is a Summary & Analysis of "The Wright Brothers" by David McCullough. You are encouraged to buy the full version.

Copyright 2015 **by** ABookADay. All rights reserved worldwide. No part of this publication may be reproduced or transmitted in any form without the prior written consent of the publisher.

TABLE OF CONTENTS

OVERVIEW

SUMMARY

PART I

Chapter 1: Beginnings

Chapter 2: The Dream Takes Hold

Chapter 3: Where the Winds Blow

Chapter 4: Unyielding Resolve

PART II

Chapter 5: December 17, 1903

Chapter 6: Out at Huffman Prairie

Chapter 7: A Capital Exhibit A

Chapter 8: Triumph at Le Mans

PART III

Chapter 9: The Crash

Chapter 10: A Time Like No Other

Chapter 11: Causes for Celebration

Epilogue

ANALYSIS

OVERVIEW

This review of the book *The Wright Brothers* by David McCullough provides a detailed summary of the book followed by an analysis. *The Wright Brothers* is an historical narrative that draws on extensive archival materials, personal journals, and public records to tell the story of the Wright brothers as men of incredible character and determination along the road towards their significant contributions to aviation history.

The summary parallels the structure of the book which is divided into three parts. The first part explores the period of the boys' childhood through their work on flight testing various models of gliders. The second part picks up with the addition of the engine to the Wright planes and traces the brother's work through the early stages of powered flight, roughly 1903 to 1908. Part three follows the brothers, now globally famous, through the years when they captured the most attention for their accomplishments. A central aspect of this historical account is the development of Orville and Wilbur Wright as individuals who showed fierce determination in the face of relentless setbacks. It also sheds light on their private nature and their deep bond as brothers.

McCullough is a two time winner of the Pulitzer Prize for other historical works, *Truman* and *John Adams*. He also won the National Book Award twice and is a recipient of the Presidential Medal of Freedom. His educational background includes a degree in English Literature from Yale University. He is also a well-known narrator, as well as previous host of *American Experience.*

SUMMARY

PART I

CHAPTER 1: BEGINNINGS

The author begins this chapter with a comparison of the two brothers in terms of their personality and habits. Wilbur is four years senior to Orville and the two were known to be inseparable. The brothers lived together, ate meals together, worked together and indeed shared even a bank account. They also shared many qualities including always dressing in professional clothes, a love for music, a penchant for cooking, a deep connection to family, a strong work ethic, a self-deprecating character and a distaste for public attention. They were both temperate and seemingly unconcerned with romance. Both had extraordinary drive and determination for their common mission. There were also differences between the brothers. Wilbur was more serious and reflective, had a stronger memory, and was more detached from the opinions of others. Orville was known to be a slightly more dapper dresser, had a gentler nature, and was shy and sensitive. Orville also excelled at mechanical ingenuity.

The author then turns to the family of the brothers. Their younger sister Katharine was the only member of the family to graduate from college. She was also quite talkative, had strong opinions and was the most social member of the family. There were also two older brothers, Reuchlin and Lorin, both of whom had married and strayed from job to job to support their families. Their mother, Susan Koerner Wright, who had died of tuberculosis in 1889, is described as painfully shy, intelligent and affectionate. She also had a mind for making things such as toys and Orville's ingenuity was thought to come from her. Their father, Bishop Milton Wright was a well-traveled minister of the United Brethren Church. He had strong opinions on both personal and political matters and shared them often.

The Bishop's work with the church caused the family to move regularly. They lived in Indiana, Ohio and Iowa until 1884 when they permanently moved to Dayton, Ohio. As a child, Wilbur was exemplary in all things from sports to academics, and there were plans for him to attend Yale University. However, he was maliciously hit in the face by another boy in a game of hockey and lost all of his upper front teeth. The boy who did it, Oliver Crook Haugh, was later executed for the murder of his family and perhaps as many as a dozen others.

The incident had a deep impact on Wilbur's life. He was in terrible pain for weeks, had false teeth made, and suffered from complications such as poor digestive and heart health. At the same time his mother's condition was worsening so plans for Yale were suspended while he stayed home to care for her and rest from his own health issues for the next three years.

Their home in Dayton was modest. It had no running water until the brothers were both in their twenties. There was no electricity, food was cooked on a wood stove and light and heat were furnished with natural gas. Furnishings in the home also stressed the bare essentials. The library, however, was extensive as Bishop Wright lauded the value of reading. The library covered a wide range of subjects including literature, philosophy, history, science and theology. Intellectual curiosity was a family value.

In 1889 Orville, with the help of Wilbur, began printing a newspaper called *West Side News* using a press he built from scrap material. By the end of the year, and with Wilbur acting as editor, the newspaper was making a profit. Within another year they had changed the name of the paper, and then switched from the newspaper business to a commercial printing operation. The brothers also became interested in bicycling at this time, which had become a bit of a national craze as well as a national controversy about safety and moral health. In 1893 the brothers opened a shop where they sold and repaired bicycles, the Wright Cycle Company. By 1895, after flagging sales rebounded, they moved the shop to a downtown space with a showroom and a machine shop. They used the shop to start designing their own bicycles. The venture turned a corner and became highly successful as a result.

Chapter 2: The Dream Takes Hold

During the summer of 1896, at the age of twenty-five, Orville contracted typhoid. He was bedridden for six weeks, during which time Wilbur read to him about a German by the name of Otto Lilienthal who had recently died as the result of a gliding accident. Beginning in 1869, Lilienthal, aided coincidently by his younger brother, was conducting gliding experiments using the shape of bird wings as a model for his "sailing machines." Most of his models were crafted from muslin material stretched over a flexible willow frame. With advances in photography, and Lilienthal's enthusiastic support of being filmed, he had become a bit of a celebrity, particularly in America.

The story reignited in Wilbur a childhood passion and during Orville's recovery he began researching bird flight with a renewed vigor and a passion that had been missing from the brother's previous business ventures. Luckily the home library had just the books concerning animal locomotion that would be critical for getting Wilbur thinking in new ways about flight. Upon recovering, Orville joined his brother and read the same books. By the time the first automobile had arrived in Dayton by the way of a homemade machine of a family friend, Wilbur was too occupied with thoughts about flying machines to pay much attention.

In May of 1899, Wilbur wrote a letter to the Smithsonian Institution requesting a list of known publications on the subject of flight. The Smithsonian sent both the list of known works and their own publications on the subject and the brothers began their serious study of flight. Several notable authors in particular influenced their understanding. Samuel Pierpont Langley who was secretary of the Smithsonian and formerly a professor of astronomy and physics at the Western University of Pennsylvania had developed, with the help of Smithsonian funding, a steam-powered unmanned machine that was launched by catapult and had flown more than a half of a mile. In addition, the work of Octave Chanute, Sir George Cayley, Sir Hiram Maxim, Thomas Edison and Alexander Graham Bell were included in the research sent to the brothers. The research on aviation thus far was also littered with expensive projects and several embarrassing and public failures as well as injury and loss of life. The press often included commentary about the absurdity of flight as a part of their commentary when covering such incidents. Despite the risk of ridicule, lack of funding, and lack of formal education, the brothers were not deterred. There were also reasons for optimism. During this time new technological inventions were happening all the time and were receiving press attention and retail success. For example, Kodak cameras, electric sewing machines and safety razors, to name just a few. In addition during this time Dayton, Ohio was highest in the country in terms of per capita patent creation, largely as a result of industry in the area.

Another resource provided by the Smithsonian was of particular interest. *L'Empire de l'Air* was an 1881 book by French author Louis Pierre Mouillard. Mouillard wrote enthusiastically about bird and insect flight and maintained that it must be possible for men to understand and harness their secrets for flight. He lauded bird watching, which Wilbur subsequently took up. By this time, the dream to fly had been firmly established. They learned the language that had thus far been used to understand the dynamics of flight. Equilibrium, or the overall balance in flight, was the chief problem. It has several components. Lift is when air moving faster over the top of the wing than the bottom lowers the pressure above the wing. Pitch is the front to back angle of the machine and roll is the left to right angle. Yaw refers to the direction the plane is pointed in terms of turning the plane. For the Wright brothers, the chief technical problem became controlling all of these aspects of equilibrium in flight. Critically, this located skill in flying as something that needed to be developed through experience. Thus, it was not just technology that was conceived as a way to approach the problem, but developing skills as pilots that also struck the men as important.

It was summer of 1899 when the brothers started building their first unmanned aircraft, a five foot structure of bamboo and paper that took the form of a biplane with double wings sitting atop of each other, inspired by the gliders of Octave Chanute. The device was a kite, and strings attached to sticks allowed the person on the ground to control the "wing warping" capabilities of the design. Although the design had some flaws, it demonstrated that the wing warping technique the brothers innovated had the capacity to create the controlled equilibrium they were seeking. They began work on a manned glider using the same principles.

In order to test their glider they would need consistent and predictable wind. Wilbur wrote the United States Weather Bureau and received weather data for over one hundred weather stations. It is from this wind data, combined with the sandy beaches needed for soft landings, that they selected Kitty Hawk, a quiet location on the North Carolina Outer Banks, as the location for their tests. The 18 foot wingspan craft was finished by August, built incidentally, for less than $15 in materials. There was but one remaining piece, the long spruce spars that would be acquired in North Carolina where the glider would be assembled.

Chapter 3: Where the Winds Blow

On September 7, 1900, Wilbur arrived in Norfolk. He was not able to find the long strips of Spruce and instead found pine and made his way down to Elizabeth City by train. The Outer Banks at this time was very remote and sparsely populated. In fact, Kitty Hawk was virtually unknown to the people in Elizabeth City and it took some doing to find Israel Perry, a boat operator that happened to be raised in Kitty Hawk and could take Wilber there. The boat was in disrepair, and the 40 mile trip was full of rough seas. After a dramatic voyage, Wilbur arrived at Kitty Hawk and made contact with William Tate, the former postmaster with whom he had had some correspondence.

Kitty Hawk at the time had around 50 houses and most of the people there were fisherman and their families who eked out a living off the land in poor conditions. Wilbur stayed at the Tate house and started setting up camp and assembling the glider nearby while awaiting Orville's arrival. He also made some adjustments to the original design since the pine planks were two feet shorter than the original design called for. It is also of note that the glider was not intended to fly without wind. Using letter archives, the author demonstrates that the point of the experiment was to work out the problem of balance first.

Adding a motor was understood as something to be undertaken once balance could be achieved and fully understood. Meanwhile, as the glider came together, the locals started showing curiosity.

On September 26 Orville arrived. The glider was nearly assembled. It had two wings over each other at 5' by 17', controls to warp the wings, a horizontal rudder, and wooden skids for both take-off and landing in the sand. It weighed 50 pounds unmanned, 190 pounds with Wilbur piloting on his stomach. Experiments began on October 3, and were at first completed by flying the soaring machine as a kite with controls operated by lines that ran to the ground. The brothers were keen to use photography to record some of the experiments as well.

The kite did fly and had tremendous pull upward. Several successful flights happened before one day, while grounded for adjustments, a gust caught the glider and blew it 20 feet away and broke it into many pieces. It took three days to reassemble the plane. Meanwhile locals started gathering to watch. When the conditions were right they did manned flights, with Wilbur in the glider at the controls and the lines still anchoring the glider from flying away.

Meanwhile Wilbur continued to study the movements of sea birds from their campsite in their down time. He compared the wing shapes of the different kinds of birds and noticed their strengths and weaknesses depending on the nature of the wind they preferred flying in. A particular favorite were gannets which have a 5-6' wingspan. The brothers could be seen by locals imitating the movements of the gannets with their arms and hands.

In mid-October, facing a pressing need to return home to attend to the bicycle shop, the brothers moved the glider to a site about 4 miles away called Kill Devil Hills with the help of a local named Bill Tate. On October 19, with Wilbur piloting, the brothers made several successful flights in their soaring machine. The brothers returned home knowing that their ideas about achieving balance had merit in practice as well as theory. Once back in Dayton, amidst the daily routines of running the bicycle shop, the brothers began planning their next trip to Kitty Hawk and commenced working on a new and improved design for their glider.

In June of 1901 the brothers, their sister Katharine and their father Bishop Wright welcomed Octave Chanute for a visit to Dayton. Chanute was an engineer by trade and also one of the leading experts worldwide on gliding aviation. He brought the brothers a gift of an anemometer so they could accurately measure wind speed. He also suggested that two men whom he had worked with accompany the next trip to Kitty Hawk. In addition the brothers hired Charles Taylor, someone that could be absolutely relied on to run the bicycle shop allowing the brothers to put more concentration on their efforts to build a flying machine.

By early July of 1901 the brothers returned to Kitty Hawk. Weather conditions were much worse, however. In torrential rain they set up camp, dug a well, and built a hangar to hold the glider. In addition to poor weather, they endured a massive mosquito invasion, something known to the area every decade or so. They persevered and were joined by the men recommended by Chanute. Edward Huffaker was a student of Chanute's and brought with him a glider that he designed, and Chanute had sponsored. The other to join the party was George Alexander Spratt, whose main qualifications were that he loved to fly and had some past medical training. Huffaker soon wore out his welcome by generally being not very helpful, while Spratt was an industrious worker and proved himself quite useful.

By July 27 the team was ready to commence with experiments. After a few failed attempts, adjustments were made to Wilbur's location on the plane and they were able to fly the glider about a hundred feet. The new glider was definitely underperforming the model from the previous year. They identified the issue as that of the camber of the wings, in other words the degree of slope on the wing that created lift. They had to essentially tear down the plane and rebuild to return the camber to much closer to the previous measurements. By

August 8, and with Octave Chanute present, the wing camber issues were solved and tests were successful, but then mechanical problems with the wing warping controls created some problems and even a small crash leaving Wilbur slightly injured. The most discouraging part of the experiments were that they seemed to prove the calculation tables that they had been working from, those compiled by Lilienthal, Langley and Chanute were incorrect, which made the problems left to solve now even more numerous.

Chapter 4: Unyielding Resolve

Dour spirits did not last long and soon the brothers were back at it in Dayton. In addition, Wilbur was invited to by Chanute to deliver an address to the Western Society of Engineers in Chicago in September. The title of his paper was "Some Aeronautical Experiments" and he was introduced by Chanute himself. It was well received and published in full or part by many important publications of the day. His talk focused on the importance of balance to flying, the essential nature of gaining skill in flying to achieve that balance, and carefully and gently alluded to errors in calculations present in Chanute's and Lilienthal's earlier work.

In the fall of 1901 the brothers set their sites on finding accurate calculations upon which to model their machine. The scientific work they did was methodical and empirical. They constructed a wind tunnel with a gas powered fan at one end of a long wooden box. They built and tested airfoils made of scrap metal in thirty-eight different shapes. Meanwhile, the long time spent on experimentation was detracting from time spent on the bicycle business. Wilbur declined Chanutes repeated offers to sponsor their work.

By August 26, 1902 they departed again for Kitty Hawk with their third machine. They spent some time improving the living conditions in the hangar at Kill Devil Hills. Spratt joined them again, although to the delight of the company Huffaker did not. The new machine was by far their biggest yet. The wings measured 32' by 5' and the glider was also the largest built thus far in the world. They flew it again first as a kite and then after success with that began manned flights, very carefully. Noteworthy is that Orville was piloting as well. A small crash during this time ended with needed repairs on the machine but no major injuries. Orville also had the idea to make the rudder movable, and with some tweaks to the design the rudder and wing warping system were both attached to a single control mechanism attached to the pilot's hips.

The group continued to grow at camp. Chanute and one of his associates Augustus Herring were there, as well as older brother Lorin Wright. Chanute and Herring tested a triplane hang glider they had designed, but it was not successful despite taking up time and attention for several days. Chanute was impressed enough with the progress the brothers were making that he made a call to the head of the Smithsonian, Samuel Langley, to update him. Langley was also at work on building a flying machine but had a much more secretive style of working. He did not openly share his findings like Chanute had encouraged the Wright brothers to do. After talking with Chanute he became interested in the work of the brothers, but was politely refused when he asked if he could visit their camp at Kitty Hawk, for reasons not known.

The brothers continued their testing for a few weeks after the others left, and bested their gliding record by hitting the 600' distance mark. The last major control problem resolved, the brothers returned home at the end of October secure in the knowledge that all that was left was to add a motor.

PART II

Chapter 5: December 17, 1903 *powered flight*

Late in 1902 the brothers enquired with automobile manufacturers to see about having a custom engine made, however, the engine specs offered were all too heavy. The brothers had no knowledge of engines, but Charlie Taylor, who was in charge of the bicycle shop in their absence, was an excellent mechanic. He was able to build the first motor within six weeks despite having limited experience with repairing automobile engines and never having built one from scratch. The finished engine weighed only 152 pounds and could deliver 8 horsepower, enough to support the 675 pounds of the piloted aircraft. Upon testing, however, the block cracked and it took an additional two months to get a new block fitted. The new engine had 12 horsepower.

Wilbur and Orville worked on designing the propellers. The problem of propellers was exceedingly difficult using the existing data, which was based on boat propellers. In addition, because so many factors were interdependent in the design, the brothers decided that they would have to settle for more empirical methods and a trial and error approach. The brothers were unable to build a mathematical model for the propellers so instead decided they would have to use a trial and error approach on the machine itself. They decided on a design that had two sets of propellers spinning in opposite directions set between the wings on either side of, and slightly behind, the pilot. The final propellers were made from laminating together three layers of spruce and then hand shaping them, and they had a diameter of 8.5' when mounted. The "Flyer" was still on skids rather than wheels. The brothers filed a patent for the machine on March 23, 1903.

Meanwhile Chanute had been promoting the brothers' work in France, although positioning them more as his collaborators or his students rather than as independents. Although unclear how they found out about it, the brothers were rightly unhappy about this unfair characterization of their work. In addition, both in talks and published papers, Chanute shared openly many of the technical details of the brothers' glider which in turn would have a profound impact on the future of French aviation. In June of 1903 Wilbur gave a talk to the Western Society of Engineers discussing the experiments from the previous fall and reemphasizing the role of pilot skill in flying. He did not speak of the engine.

Meanwhile, word from Bill Tate at Kitty Hawk arrived that a gasoline tank was ready for use at the camp. Then on July 14 there was news that Samuel Langley, sponsored by $70,000 of money from the Smithsonian, the U.S. War Department and private donations, was to test what was called "The Great Aerodrome." After some weather delays on the initial launch an unmanned quarter-scale model of the machine crashed after soaring 1,000' and the press declared it a failure. By September 18 of that year, the latest Wright flying machine complete with engine and propellers departed for Kitty Hawk in carefully packed pieces.

The brothers first assembled the glider from the previous year and practiced over 75 glides. Then they erected a 16' by 44' hangar for the new plane before beginning the plane assembly. Fierce winds slowed the progress. Meanwhile on October 7, Langley had launched the full scale Aerodrome and it had immediately crashed in the Ocean. A month later the brothers' plane was nearing full assembly, however, upon starting the engine some misfiring due to mechanical failure damaged the propeller shafts which had to be shipped back to Charlie Taylor at the bicycle shop. Near the end of November new heavier steel propeller shafts arrived, but cracked upon testing. Orville returned to Dayton with the broken propellers.

On December 8 the Langley ship was ready for another launch. With Charles Manly as the pilot the ship was launched by catapult and immediately broke apart and fell into the icy sea. Again the crash was very public and the press rather mercilessly chided Langley's efforts, even going so far as to call for the government to withdrawal its funds. Langley died three years later, still riddled with humiliation. The Wright brothers, in communications with others, focused on the contributions of Langley's work to the field of aeronautics and remarked that the press had been overly harsh in judging his body of work.

On December 11 Orville returned to Kitty Hawk with the new solid steel propeller shafts. On the 14th they were ready for the first test and they positioned the plane on the 60' wood launching track they had constructed. After winning a coin toss, Wilbur boarded the machine as pilot. Wilbur inclined the plane too steeply, followed by an over correction, causing the plane to crash not far off the end of the track. However, damage was minor and the overall sense was that the machine was indeed operational once Wilbur adjusted to the controls. In two days, repairs were done.

The morning of December 17 was bitter cold. Only five people came to see the launch that day, and notably none of them were from the press. Wind was not ideal and had a gale force of 20 to 27 miles per hour which would make it difficult to find balance. This time, Orville would pilot the plane. At 10:35 the Flyer started down the runway, and at the end of the runway one of the helpers, Daniels, snapped a picture of the Flyer lifting off the ground. The plane flew an erratic 120 feet before digging one wing into the sand and coming to a stop. The next launch had Wilbur flying for 175', then Orville for 200'. On the fourth test Wilbur piloted the craft for a half a mile. Then the Flyer was caught by the wind while on the ground and swept up and over several times with Daniels caught up in the wires. No one was badly injured. No matter, the first flights in the world from a powered piloted machine were now accomplishments to belong forever to the Wright brothers and their Flyer. The Flyer, incidentally, would be packed up and stored, never to be flown again.

Chapter 6: Out at Huffman Prairie

Upon receiving a telegram of the flight, their sister Katharine notified their brother Lorin, who informed the *Dayton Daily Journal* of the feat. Unfortunately the editor was not impressed with the news and the flight duration of 57 seconds, and the story got buried to an inside page of the *Journal*. In addition, the operator that sent the original telegram from the Kitty Hawk weather station leaked the telegram to the *Virginian-Pilot* who invented a largely erroneous story based on very little factual information. Subsequent newspapers further embellished. The Cabot family, wealthy brothers from Boston, took note of the story, however, and contacted the Wright brothers. They had a distant family relation in Senator Henry Cabot Lodge from Massachusetts, whom they pressured to make the work of the Wrights known to President Roosevelt. The Senator's efforts got stalled at the War Department. Essentially no big deal was made about the accomplishments of the Wright brothers' Flyer. So they went back to work in the bicycle shop in Dayton, Ohio making improvements to the machine.

There were, however, money problems. Up to this point the efforts of the brothers was entirely funded from the modest income of the bicycle shop. Since the brothers were now interested in building a larger plane with a larger motor, the income from the bicycle shop alone would not be enough to continue the work. One decision that was made to cut expenses was to move the experimental station closer to home rather than incurring the considerable expenses of moving the machine. Huffman Prairie was an 84 acre cow field only about eight miles from Dayton that was selected for the new experimental flying grounds. The ground required work to get it into shape due to the groundhogs on the property. The brothers themselves set about the field flattening groundhog mounds and clearing small brush. By spring of 1904 they were ready to test a new machine, the Flyer II.

On May 26 they flew Flyer II in front of spectators and members of the press, but the flight was only a few seconds long, and only 8 feet off the ground, as something had failed with the engine. For the next three months many such mishaps occurred during the experiments. The brothers persevered and on August 13, with Wilbur at the controls, they flew over 1000 feet.

A chief problem that became apparent from the new location was that the wind was less reliable. The brothers decided they needed to be free of the wind for launching and built a gravity operated catapult with a 1,600 pound weight dropped from a 20' tower, and a pulley system that would launch the plane on a flat track. The system, the first test of which was September 7, was a huge success effectively making wind a nonissue for take-off. On September 15 Wilbur flew a half mile and completed a half circle turn. Meanwhile, there was not much local attention or publicity generated over the achievements. The author suggests that the reporters in town did not believe that the brothers were flying their machine and, incredibly, they did not bother to go out to the field to see for themselves.

On September 20, 1904 a man by the name of Amos Ives Root, now independently wealthy after becoming known as the "bee man" of Ohio, was invited to visit Huffman Prairie for a second visit to the Flyer II trials. A machine enthusiast himself, he would become the champion of the Wright brothers, lauding both the importance of their technical achievements and their incredible ingenuity. He recounted what he saw in his own publication, *Gleanings in Bee Culture*. What he witnessed that day was Wilbur flying the Flyer II in a full circle with a soft landing. His account also included praise and understanding concerning the skill that the brothers had in flying the machine. In addition, Root was a car enthusiast and had a knack for understanding the transportation value of flying machines. The article was published in January of 1905 and at the same time was offered to the *Scientific American*, which turned it down and instead, a few months later, published a story casting doubt that any such flying was even happening.

In October of 1904 a British Army officer named Lieutenant Colonel John Edward Capper came to visit the brothers and upon meeting them, and without seeing the Flyer II in action, asked them if they would be interested in selling the Flyer II to the British government. They turned that offer down. In January of 1905 they sent a letter to Congressman Robert Nevin, who forwarded it to the War Department, who forwarded it to the Board of Ordnance and Fortification, explaining their successes. The reply was a form rejection letter. It is not clear why, although the author speculates as to several possible reasons including that the department having lost the $50,000 invested in Langley's very public failure, the flooding of the department with other crank proposals, a general sense that flying was just impossible, or perhaps simple ineptitude. After the rejection, the brothers started corresponding with Colonel Capper to revisit sale of the machine to Great Britain.

Meanwhile the brothers started work on the Flyer III, with practicality being a chief concern in the design. It had a more powerful engine at 25 horsepower, slightly redesigned wings, and a larger rudder that was moved forward in the design. By June of 1905, they were testing the Flyer III. They started having longer flights up to 15 miles, and flights were now long enough for the brothers to both increase their skill at flying tremendously. They started inviting family and friends out to the fields and on October 5 flew around the field 29 times in front of at least twelve witnesses. Again they appealed to Washington and again they were denied, despite now making regular flights over 25 miles long.

Having received no interest on multiple occasions to sell the plane to America, and having stalled on talks with the British, the brothers struck a deal with a Frenchman named Arnold Fordyce who was interested in purchasing the plane as a gift to the French government for a sum of $200,000 pending testing of the aircraft.

Chapter 7: A Capital Exhibit A

On March 20, 1906, Arnold Fordyce, accompanied by three French Army officers dressed in plain clothes and American attorney, Walter Berry, came to Dayton to verify that the Flyer III could perform to the specifications of the sale contract. The first meetings took place in the bicycle shop for over two weeks. Because the brothers were concerned about having their ideas stolen, they shared photographs and eye witness testimony of their flights, but did not show the Flyer III. Although the deal had been strengthened, it had not been finalized.

There was also a sea change occurring in terms of how the brothers were received by the American press. The April 7, 1906 edition of the *Scientific American* had a lengthy article that included various eye witness testimony as to the long and controlled flights they had seen. Additionally, in May 1906, the patent on the Wright Flying Machine was issued. And in France, a pilot by the name of Alberto Santos-Dumont made a 726 flight in his powered machine.

Then an offer came from Flint & Company, which was a company out of New York which offered $500,000 for rights to sell the plane in non-U.S. markets and allowing the Wright brothers control of any U.S. sales. The brothers were still in negotiations with the firm when they were asked to go to Europe to meet Hart O. Berg, the Flint & Company's representative in Europe who was skeptical about the claims of the Flyer III. So, for the first time being separated from his family for an extended period of time, Wilbur Wright set sail on May 18 for Europe.

The two businessmen met in London and made haste to Paris. Berg was an arms merchant that had contacts with government officials highly located across Europe. He was also an American, having a background in engineering. Another executive from Flint, Frank Cordley, met them on route to Paris. In his down time, Wilbur visited the many museums and sites of Paris, reveling in the architecture, art and historical features. Berg arranged many meetings with highly located private businessmen interested in aviation as well as government officials. The author goes into detail about Wilbur's demeanor during the twists and turns of the negotiations. The general sentiment here is that Wilbur handled himself well despite the tedious process of ongoing negotiations with various stakeholders. He also grew in confidence as the trip wore on that he had a handle on the situation. One key bottom line of the negotiations was that no deal would be complete until the Flyer III had a public demonstration in France as there were still several important figures who were highly skeptical as to the truth of the Wright brothers' claims.

Meanwhile, due in large part to a sense of powerless over negotiations and general anxiety as to the current progress, things with the family back in Dayton were deteriorating. Tension was high in the family, and Orville was so distraught with angst he had stopped working. A growing distrust from the family members back home concerning Flint & Company, possibly due to anti-Semitism, was also a contributing factor. Despite his disheveled mental state, Orville headed to Paris with the Flyer III disassembled and shipped to a customs house in Paris. The brothers met in Paris in late July and the tension between them soon dissipated.

The next day the brothers had an intense meeting with executives from Flint & Company and stood firm on their position that that they would retain ownership of the patent, and that Flint & Company were merely sales agents, which assuaged most of Orville's concerns that the company was trying to hedge in as partners. And, with interest in France waning due to the August vacationing time, Wilbur went to Germany with Berg and Orville stayed in Paris to greet the arrival of Charlie Taylor. By mid-August progress had stalled with both the Germans and the French. They took to enjoying the parks in Paris and playing the child's game called diablo where, with a string and two sticks, the player mastered keeping a spool in the air. They played the game publically and this added to the press' sense of mystery about these American men.

By the beginning of November, with no firm deals in place, the brothers decided it was time to return to Dayton. Before leaving they were invited to see the French pilot Henri Farman. The brothers did not seem concerned about the aviator in terms of competition. Nor were they seemingly bothered by a host of other French aviators such as Gabriel and Charles Voisin, Léon Delagrange, Santos-Dumont, Comte Charles de Lambert or Louis Blériot. The brothers returned home to Dayton with plans to continue building flying machines and plans to visit Europe again the following spring if nothing came along from the U.S. Government. They left the Flyer III at the customs house in Paris.

On the way home Wilbur stopped through Washington D.C. and reported home that at long last the U.S. Government was showing interest in their planes. In the first months of 1908 the brothers had a contract with the U.S. War Department for $25,000 for a Flyer, and a contract with a French company by the name of La Comagnie Générale de Navigation Aérienne pending demonstrations in France.

Chapter 8: Triumph at Le Mans

By spring of 1908 it was abundantly clear that the brothers, who had not actually flown in nearly two years, would need to practice to be ready for the public demonstrations that were now imperative for finalizing their business arrangements. They decided to return to Kitty Hawk, and found the Devil Hills camp in ruin. Wilbur arrived first and set about essentially building the camp from scratch.

The new Flyer featured side by side pilot seats to allow for betting control of the wing warping system. Three weeks after Wilbur arrived the *Virginian-Pilot* invented a story about the Wright brothers return to Kitty Hawk that featured an all-out fabrication of a ten mile flight that started to draw reporters to the remote island. On May 6 flight tests commenced. Taking turns the brothers flew several flights. More reporters started to arrive and could be seen scouting from the scrub brush on the hillsides surrounding the test area. The first published photograph of a Wright brother's Flyer was taken by photographer James Hare from *Collier's Weekly*.

The brothers had decided not to ever fly together in the plane for fear of a crash. They wanted to be sure that one brother would be able to carry on their important work. On May 14 Wilbur made a mistake at the controls causing a crash in which he had to be pulled from the plane wreckage. Although he was injured, and the plane was destroyed, there were no broken bones. This brought the Kitty Hawk trials to an end. The brothers decided that Wilbur would travel to France for the required demonstrations there, and Orville would fly the Washington demonstrations.

Meanwhile, there had been much ado about several recent flights in France including a two minute flight by Henri Farman and several demonstrations by Delagrange. Meanwhile Wilbur and Berg went to the town of Le Mans where a wealthy balloon enthusiast and auto manufacturer named Léon Bollée had suggested there was plenty of usable flat land for their demonstrations. Bollée donated some of his nearby factory space to assemble the Flyer, some help from his workers, and arranged for the nearby Hunaudières racetrack as a site for the trials. Wilbur gave his first interview to the French press to a journalist named François Peyrey who would write quite a bit of Wilbur in the coming months.

On June 16 Wilbur started to unpack the Flyer and found it in very bad shape. Assuming that the damage was due to poor packing, he wrote Orville an angry letter at once, only to find out later that it was the French customs inspectors that had done the damage. Wilbur set about fixing the plane with some help from Bollée's mechanics (who did not speak English). On Sundays he did not work and his letters from this time again focus on the architecture of the town of Le Mans that quite impressed him.

On July 4 while testing the engine, a steam hose broke free and scalded Wilbur badly along his arm and chest. Bollée happened to be in the shop and got help quickly. Although he downplayed the accident to the family back home, he was unable to use his left arm for a month which slowed progress on assembly. By early August the plane was assembled, however with several adjustments made necessary by the poor condition of the machine. On August 6 it was moved in secret to a shed by the racetrack where Wilbur would sleep.

On August 8, 1908 the stands at the racetrack filled with people from the town of Le Mans, various press, as well as some notable guests including a few uniformed Russian officers, Ernest Archdeacon who was a prominent member of the Aéro-Club de France, and the famous French aviator, Louis Blériot. Archdeacon was notoriously and publically very skeptical of the Wright brothers and their flying machine. A loudspeaker announced that no photographs were permitted. At three O'clock the Flyer was brought out of the shed and Wilbur proceeded, in no particular hurry, to check every aspect of the track and the catapult system. At six-thirty he turned to the men aiding him on the track and said "Gentlemen, I'm going to fly."

He got into the plane but after the engines started got out to make one last check before being catapulted into the air, making a graceful turn heading back to the grandstand, then circling again. He flew about two miles in as many minutes. The crowd went wild. Even the other pilots that were there were very impressed and stated that they understood that Wilbur and the Flyer were both far beyond the French in terms of aviation. By the next day the press on a global scale reported enthusiastically of the success of the flight. French aviators and aviation enthusiasts also expressed public and broad support. Including Archdeacon who immediately after the demonstration admitted he had been completely wrong about the brothers. What was noted by those in attendance was not the duration of the flight, but the clear absolute control that Wilbur Wright had of the machine which stood in stark contrast to the other flying demonstrations up to this point.

The following Monday, after resting on Sunday as was the Wright family custom, the demonstrations resumed, this time to a crowd of at least two thousand people. After marching into the grandstand to take a forbidden camera away from a French Army Captain, Wilbur performed two flights, the second with a figure 8 maneuver followed by landing in the precise position from which he took off. He flew again on August 13, and performed several circles around the field. This time after one turn he made a mistake and came in too low and a tip of the wing hit the ground. He was not injured despite the accident, and the spectators thought him no less a genius even with this mistake. The matter had been settled in France, the Wright brothers were acknowledged as the originators of the first true flying machine. The *Dayton Herald* also wrote stories hailing the brothers as local heroes. The French Army suggested a larger field about seven miles east called Camp d'Auvours and on August 21 he began trials there to growing crowds. Meanwhile, as Orville prepared for similar demonstrations in Washington D.C., Wilbur wrote to caution his brother to be safe, cautious and to not be pressured by the enthusiasm of the onlookers to take unnecessary risks.

PART III

CHAPTER 9: THE CRASH

The American demonstrations would take place in Fort Myer, Virginia. There was a shed ample to house and work on the plane, but the field itself was fairly tight. With help from Charlie Taylor and Charlie Furnas, on September 3 the Flyer was ready for the first trial. Orville was markedly nervous and the press of journalists was constant. The first flight was less than a minute and shaky. The next day Orville circled the field several times and had more control. Subsequent flights were also successful and started to draw wide attention from the press.

On the morning of September 9, 1908 Orville was in the air nearly an hour circling the field 56 times. News went out that he would fly again in the afternoon and many Washington offices closed so people could go and see the afternoon demonstration. Orville then circled the field another 55 times, and was in the air for 63 minutes, a new world record. On September 10, he went around 57.5 times for a total of 66 minutes in the air. The next day, a 70 minute flight adding several tricky maneuvers of low flights and tight turns. By the

12th of September the crowd was numbered around 5000 spectators. Both of the brothers were inundated with attention, and since they were both rather private men, the attention was tolerated at best, but not welcomed.

On September 17 a demonstration was planned at Fort Myer with a passenger, Army officer Lieutenant Thomas Selfridge. Selfridge had some level of expertise in aeronautics, and was a member of the Aerial Experiment Association (AEA) which was headed by Alexander Graham Bell. There was some distrust on the part of Orville with Selfridge due to the concern that the AEA might have commercial interests in knowing the proprietary secrets of the Wright brothers Flyer. He was also the heaviest passenger they had tested in the plane at 175 pounds. The flight started well enough, however, after the third time around the field something went wrong. Some debris came off the plane into the air and shortly after the plane started to violently shake. Orville turned off the engine and prepared for a gliding landing but then suddenly the plane took a nose dive and slammed into the ground from about 75 feet in the air.

The crowd rushed the field and had to be held back with cavalrymen. The men were pulled from the wreckage and dashed to the nearby hospital. It was not until much later that evening that a report was issued that Orville was alive but in critical condition. He had fractured his hip and legs and suffered four broken ribs. Selfridge had died from a fractured skull. Despite the crash, the success of the previous demonstrations had made clear that aviation was possible and that the Wright brothers could be credited with the success of designing the first viable powered plane technology.

Upon hearing the news, Katharine immediately set off for Washington. The news was delivered to Wilbur, who was still at Le Mans, by Hart Berg. He postponed all demonstrations for a week and refused any visitors with the exception of a few close friends. Accounts from the time suggest that he felt a tremendous sense of guilt for not being with his brother to have helped in the preflight inspection and other safety measures. By the week's end it was clear that Orville would heal from his injuries, although certainly a pall was cast because of Selfridge's death. Wilbur was not deterred from the rest of his demonstrations. On September 21 he resumed in front of a crown of 10,000 spectators and flew a new world record of 40 miles in 91 minutes and 25 seconds.

Meanwhile Orville's progress was slow. His leg was broken in two places and held in a sling suspended from the ceiling. Katharine spent a great deal of time with him at the hospital and kept Wilbur informed of the details of his recovery. The cause of the crash had also been determined upon examination of the wreckage. A propeller blade had cracked and became entangled in the wires that braced the rudders.

The plane was locked down and guarded in the shed on the field. On September 23, however, Alexander Graham Bell with two members of the AEA were able to gain access to the plane without anyone from the Wright team knowing about it and took at least one measurement of the wings. Meanwhile, Katharine kept vigil and handled visitors and journalists as well as correspondence for Orville during his recuperation.

On October 31, not fully recovered yet, it was decided that getting Orville back home to Dayton would help his recovery. A crowd at the train station saw him off. By mid-November Orville was visiting the shop in Dayton by wheelchair and plans were being made for him and Katharine to join Wilbur in France.

Chapter 10: A Time Like No Other

In France, Wilbur Wright was a sensation. Over 200,000 spectators had seen his demonstrations along with several famous passengers. He was given numerous awards, including the prestigious Gold Medal award from the Aéro-Club at a huge banquet in his honor, and indeed the French Legion of Honor was awarded to both brothers. The French contract requirements had been met with the demonstrations and now was left the matter of training three French aviators. The first of such was Comte Charles de Lambert. The Flyer was fitted with a second set of controls so that the copilot could fly the plane and Wilbur could take over if need be.

With winter coming Wilbur decided to move the training ground to a resort town named Pau, which had both better weather this time of year, and was closer to the home town of de Lambert. The location was also well known for attracting many people from the highest echelon of society. December 31, despite cold rain, Wilbur did his last event at Le Mans where he took off without the catapult and flew 77 miles in 140 minutes, winning the Michelin Cup, a prize recently set up by the new tire company.

Katharine, accompanying Orville who was now walking with the aid of a cane, boarded a ship for France on January 5,

1909. She was greeted six days later by Wilbur and the Bergs in Paris. They followed Wilbur to Pau, and all but Wilbur stayed at the luxurious Grand Hôtel Gassion with a view of the Pyrénées. Wilbur stayed at Pont-Long about six miles away, the field that he and de Lambert had chosen for training. The Wrights were apparently the main subject of conversation in Pau that year. As the weather got warmer still, English royalty abounded in the area as well as French dignitaries, and American millionaires. At one point, former prime minister of England, Arthur Balfour, was on hand to help load the catapult. The king of Spain, Alfonso XIII cane to witness the flights in February. Meanwhile the press worldwide was on hand to document their adventures. Orville was not able to help with the demonstrations or preparations much due to his physical condition, and he was largely silent to the press. Katharine was well liked by the press and was more willing to talk with them.

Training of de Lambert and the two other French aviators, Paul Tissandier and Paul N. Lucas-Girardville continued at the field. Additional passengers were also given rides, including Katharine. On March 17 the King of England, Edward VII, at 68 years old, arrived at Pau. He was taken for a tour of the Flyer, and also the new Flyer being assembled at the field, and given a special demonstration of the plane in flight. In the afternoon of the same day, de Lambert successfully performed his first solo flight.

The press in America too was following the brothers and all of their accomplishments. Numerous awards were planned. Dayton too made plans for a huge celebration for the brothers upon their return. There was also great movement of other accomplishments elsewhere in the aviation world. France had as many as fifteen airplane factories in operation at this time, new aviation prizes were being developed, and aviation themed publications had exploded in number.

Preparations were made to go to Rome. The new Flyer was packed and shipped and the old Flyer stayed in Paris eventually to find its way into a museum there. By the time they got to Rome, the city was full of tourists, many of whom were Americans. Here Wilbur flew many successful flights and trained Italian aviators in front of huge crowds. He also took a journalist into the air who took the first motion picture films from a plane in history. After over a year in Europe, Wilbur would return to America with Katharine and Orville on May 5.

Chapter 11: Causes for Celebration

On May 13, 1909 the brothers and their sister arrived at the train station in Dayton to a huge crowd of enthusiastic supporters. Factory whistles blew, cannons fired, and carriages drawn by white horses awaited to take them and several town officials to their home on Hawthorn Street. Along the ride cheering crowds filled the street. More than 10,000 people gathered in the streets outside their home. The Mayor announced a huge city wide celebration, and Orville announced that he would soon return to flying at Fort Meyer. The brothers were also anxious to start working on the next Flyer.

On June 10 the brothers and Katharine went to Washington D.C. to receive two Gold Medals from the Aero Club of America presented by President Taft at the White House. By day's end they were back on a train to Dayton where the city celebrations awaited them. On June 17 the two day city wide commemoration of the Wright brothers commenced. The festivities were colossal. A great parade of floats depicted the history of the town through the ages, ending with a half size replica of a Flyer. 560 costumed people representing the different periods joined the parade. Great columns lined the streets with colored lights, bands played, firemen and soldiers marched. A living flag made up of 2,500 children dressed in red, white and blue covered the Fair Grounds. Businesses closed and the keys to the city were presented to the brothers. Meanwhile, and rather miraculously, the brothers managed to slip away and make some time to work during the festivities. As soon as the celebrations were over, the brothers went to Fort Myers near Washington to resume flying trials.

The trials were scheduled to start on June 26 and a crowd of about 4,000, including many high ranking military officials and senators, waited in unbearable heat for hours before the trials were called that day due to high winds. The brothers did not want to test a brand new machine in less than ideal conditions. On the 29th conditions were good enough for flying, and Orville flew a few flights where the machine underperformed but the brothers were confident that the machine would perform once they fine-tuned it and Orville got used to the way the new machine handled. However, the engine was having some troubles. On July 2 the engine cut off midair and although Orville was able to glide the plane to a landing, two skids were broken and the wing badly torn. He was not hurt. Undeterred the brothers and Charlie continued to work on the plane and the trials continued. On July 25 came news that Louis Blériot had crossed the English Channel.

By July 27 the new Flyer was performing better and Orville, accompanied by Lieutenant Frank Lahm, set a new world endurance record flying at 150', for 79 times around the field for a total duration of 72 minutes. President Taft was among the spectators that day. On July 30 Orville successfully flew a speed trial set by the U.S. Army, winning a $30,000 contract with the War Department.

In August the first international air race was being sponsored in Reims, France. Twenty-two pilots would compete. Charles de Lambert and Paul Tissandier were flying Wright planes built by the French. In addition, the American pilot, Glenn Curtiss, participated on behalf of the American Aero club but only after the Wright brothers made clear they could not attend. Curtiss would win the race for speed in a plane built by his company. Meanwhile Wilbur stayed back in the States to tend to a lawsuit concerning patent infringement against the Herring-Curtiss Company.

Orville headed to Germany for some trial flights and attracted an audience of as many as 200,000. Wilbur decided to fly his first U.S. public demonstration. He would fly in New York at a gathering that was celebrating the 300th anniversary of Hudson's traversing of the Hudson River, and the 100th anniversary of Robert Fulton's Hudson steamboat. Glenn Curtiss, now famous in America for his performance at Reims, would also be part of the celebration. In order to prepare for an emergency landing over the water, Wilbur had a canoe attached to the bottom of the Flyer. On a test flight in preparation for the big flight along the Hudson River, Wilbur took a detour and did a circle around the Statue of Liberty and a rather large deal was made of it by the press. While waiting for the weather to improve to fly the Hudson River, news arrived that Orville had flown to 984' in the air, a new world record, while in Germany. Meanwhile Curtiss, needing to attend to other matters, had to leave New York. On October 4 Wilbur made the flight up the Hudson River, staying at a low elevation due to the strong air currents created by the sky scrapers. Although an afternoon flight was also planned, it had to be cancelled due to a blown piston in the engine.

On October 18, Katharine and Orville were in Paris, a stop they were making on their way home from Germany. Unbeknownst to all but a scant few, de Lambert surprised the city of Paris with a fly over in a Wright biplane. He even flew over the Eiffel tower, which was at that time the tallest man made structure at an elevation of 986'. Upon landing he credited the success of the flight with the Wright brothers' plane.

The next year filled with the details of incorporating a Wright Company for the manufacturing of planes, and enforcing their many patents. An office was set up in New York City. Unfortunately, longtime friend Octave Chanute fell on the other side of some patent disagreements, in particular their invention of the wing warping system, and their relationship became severely strained.

On May 25, 1910 Orville and Wilbur planned some demonstration flights for spectators out at Huffman Prairie. Orville did most of the flying, doing many impressive maneuvers including climbing to a height of 2,720'. In addition, the Wright brothers took a flight together, something they had never done before. And, for the first time, Orville took his father, Bishop Wright, into the air.

EPILOGUE

Wilbur took on the bulk of the work in the patent lawsuits. The author here argues that it was not the money that concerned the brothers so much as protecting their legacy as the inventors of the airplane. He would take only one other flight after the flight he shared with his brother at Huffman Prairie. He died at age forty-five from typhoid on May 30, 1912. His father out lived him for five years and lived with Katharine and Orville. Katharine devoted much of her time to causes such as women's suffrage and to her Alma Matter Oberlin College. She also helped Orville and they traveled to Europe again. In 1926, at age fifty-eight, she announced plans to wed that so upset Orville he refused to see her until upon her death bed in March of 1929.

Orville continued fly the new models of Wright planes until 1918, despite a nearly fatal crash in 1914. Eventually however, the old wounds from the crash at Fort Meyers were enough to stop his flying career. In 1918 he also sold the Wright Company and instead placed his energy into the Wright Aeronautical Laboratory. He also oversaw several lawsuits during that time. And, much to his great disappointment, the case of Samuel Langley and his Aerodrome was reopened by the Smithsonian with the help of Glenn Curtiss. Curtiss made several undisclosed modifications to the original ship and after a 1914 test of the machine the Smithsonian declared that it was Langley that built the first airship with the capacity to carry a person for a sustained flight. In addition, Orville was disheartened by the role of bombers and the destruction and loss of life they created during WWI. He also lived to see the growth of aviation to include jet technology, rockets and breaking the sound barrier. He died on January 30, 1948 after having outlived his older brother by thirty-six years.

ANALYSIS

The Wright Brothers is a deftly written book. Prolific author, David McCullough, offers the reader a glimpse into the day to day lives of Orville and Wilbur Wright, a perspective that is often over shadowed in other accounts that focus heavily on the technical accomplishments of these innovators. McCullough is a master storyteller and expert historian, drawing on a seemingly endless array of primary source material from archives, museums, correspondence, journals, published news and public records. Despite a fine grain detail on the particulars of daily life, the narrative is strong enough to carry the reader through and create a sense of excitement about what will happen next.

A particular strength of the book is that the reader will come to understand how critical the personal character of these men was to their eventual success in aviation. Part of that traces to the context the author provides concerning the overwhelming doubt among many experts and lay people alike as to even the possibility of flight, particularly during the early period of the brothers' work. Despite many setbacks in a climate where even investing time in aviation was viewed as madness by many, the brothers persevered despite limited financial resources and a lack of valid empirical data from which to build a functional

Flyer. The author reveals there is greatness in the details of mundane life demonstrated not just by the successes along the way, but also the string of unsatisfactory trials that the brothers treated as opportunities for understanding, ultimately mastering the dynamics of powered flight where many before had failed.

The book also reveals that the Wright family, in particular their sister Katharine and father Bishop Wright, were instrumental to the brothers' accomplishments. For example, by highlighting the many roles of Katharine in terms of helping to manage affairs at home, caring for the needs of Orville after his crash in 1908, and her work handling correspondence and other social coordination duties creates a sense that the brothers' work might not have been enabled without that considerable support. This is a departure from stories that locate the Wright brothers as islands of intellectual or mechanical prowess. A more accurate picture emerges of extraordinary men of both talent and character with a supportive family capable of providing guidance, assistance, and support of various kinds. Given that neither brother would marry, and that both lived a considerable majority of their lives under the same roof with sister and father, this family unit was not a trivial part of their story, and McCullough's telling reflects that fact.

The book is somewhat more forthcoming about Wilbur than Orville. This may be in part due to the availability of archival resources, or it may simply be because Wilbur was in many ways the more public of the brothers. In any case, there is a sense that many readers will have after reading the book that Orville remains a bit of a mystery. Lacking as well are more technical aspect of the brothers' work, although this is covered in more detail in other books, and certainly part of the strength of this volume is that the author has avoided getting too mired down in details of theory. Still, some readers may be disappointed in the balance the author has struck. Another downside to the book is that the photograph plates are sequestered at the end of the book. It would have added significant value if the illustrations lived next to the vivid descriptions the author provides.

Overall, this book is a must read for enthusiasts of aviation history and those that have a passion for learning about the lives of historical figures alike. With rich detail, a robust attention to context, and a superb narrative style, *The Wright Brothers* is unlikely to disappoint.

Made in the USA
Middletown, DE
09 January 2017